Michael O. Amamieye

7 Days to Conquer your Fears

Unless otherwise stated, all scripture quotations are from the King James Version of the Bible.

Reprinted 2020

Published by:

MAWO Prints

Plot 13 Walter Akpana Lay Out off 394 Ikwerre Road Mile 5 Rumueprikom,

P. O. Box 12378, Port Harcourt, Nigeria.

E-mail: info@aggressivefaith.org

Website: www.aggressivefaith.org

Phones: +2349018006296, +2348050987377, WhatsApp:+2348036732188

U.S.A.: +1-916-245-6157

ISBN: 978-978-51071-4-2

Printed in the Federal Republic of Nigeria

Table of Content

Dedication 7

Preface 9

What is Man? 18

Commitment 38

Day One 42

Day Two 50

Day Three 57

Day Four 64

Day Five 71

Day Six 78

Day Seven 84

DEDICATION

I dedicate this devotional to my daughters:

Edwina Aleme

Tracy Nicholas

Mehetabel Favour

I see you rise above fear to become all that God has designed you to be in your life time.

PREFACE

The mind is the mould for everything man has created. Nothing becomes a reality until it has been processed and packaged in the mind. If your mind can change, then, your mouth and every other thing you see around you can change.

"And God said, Let us make man in our image, after our likeness: and let them have dominion over the fish of the sea, and over the fowl of the air, and over the cattle, and over all the earth, and over every creeping thing that creepeth upon the earth." Gen. 1:26.

Two things you will notice that make man look like God: image and likeness. The word, *image*,

Hebrew **tselem** is a painting that represents the original. It is a shadow of the real. It is the ghost of the substance. Because God is Spirit, everything in His world exist first in the spirit world before they become manifest in any other realm.

Man is essentially a spirit being like God. Before he is born or begins to exist in any realm, he has been in existence in the spirit realm. This means that for him to manufacture or manifest anything in his world, he must first produce a painting or shadow or ghost of that thing. That is why before man builds anything, he first creates a mold or model or image.

Think until it becomes a ghost.

Think until it becomes a mold.

Think until it becomes a model.

Think until it becomes an image.

The other word is, *likeness*, Hebrew **demut**. It means a pattern, figure, form or shape. Man just like God can manufacture or manifest anything that he has been able to like or describe or desire to the extent that he has been able to give it a shape or size. If you can describe something that you desire so much so that it is real to you, you can reproduce it. The power of desire and description go together to form this likeness.

Think until you can sketch a pattern in your mind and on paper.

Think until you can figure out the different shapes and sizes.

Think until you can formulate the distinct colors.

Think until you can desire it with every emotion you can muster.

Think until you can describe it with such specifics and emotions.

Both image and likeness are formed in the mind or soul. When God formed man, he became a living soul – a mind with the same capacity like God to create his world.

"And the Lord God formed man of the dust of the ground, and breathed into his nostrils the breath of life; and man became a living soul." Gen. 2:7.

A living soul is that part of man that is alive to its creative capacity. With this part of being, man is just like God. He can think like God. He can talk like God. He can act like God. He can see the same results that God can. However, he becomes dangerous and evil when he is disconnected from God. This is why when man sinned against God, he was still like God in the sense that he can create but then, his creativity became perverted.

A perversion is a twisted form of the original. It works in the opposite direction. It becomes an opposition. ***"And the Lord God said, Behold, the man is become as one of us, to know good and evil…"*** Gen. 3:22. The perversion heightens the evil desires and descriptions to the exclusions of the good.

Just as it is impossible to stop God from creating good even so it becomes almost impossible to stop the perverted mind from creating evil. The only way to stop evil from becoming a reality is to stop the mind from painting the images. The painting is done by words because words are spirits reflecting the nature of his being. **So if you stop the words**

that paint the pictures, you can stop the pictures from becoming a reality.

For the next Seven Days, I want to help you paint the picture of your future. The guaranty you have is that NOTHING will be restrained from you if you can imagine it in your mind, speak it with your mouth and take corresponding actions that will create your reality.

"And the Lord said, Behold, the people is one, and they have all one language; and this they begin to do: and now nothing will be restrained from them, which they have imagined to do." Gen. 11:6.

WHAT IS MAN?

Man is a six days being because he was created on the sixth day. His number is six because anything man can do consistently for six days can become perfected on the seventh day. *"Here is wisdom. Let him that hath understanding count the number of...man; and his number is Six..."* Rev. 13:18.

"And God said, Let us make man in our image, after our likeness: and let them have dominion over the fish of the sea, and over the fowl of the air, and over the cattle, and over all the earth, and over every creeping thing that creepeth upon the earth.

27 So God created man in his own image, in the image of God created he him; male and female created he them.

28 And God blessed them, and God said unto them, Be fruitful, and multiply, and replenish the earth, and subdue it: and have dominion over the fish of the sea, and over the fowl of the air, and over every living thing that moveth upon the earth.

29 And God said, Behold, I have given you every herb bearing seed, which is upon the face of all the earth, and every tree, in the which is the fruit of a tree yielding seed; to you it shall be for meat.

30 And to every beast of the earth, and to every fowl of the air, and to every thing that creepeth upon the earth, wherein there is life, I have given every green herb for meat: and it was so.

31 And God saw every thing that he had made, and, behold, it was very good. And the evening and the morning were the sixth day." Gen. 1:26-31.

"What is man, that thou art mindful of him? and the son of man, that thou visitest him?" Psalm 8:4.

That is a question when you understand will change the way you look at yourself. The Hebrew word, **adam**, used for man means a human being with blood. The blood which is red in some other expressions defines man as red. That is why the verb, **adom**, which means to be red implies the original ruddiness of man because it is the blood that makes man both alive and real. Every human being has in them blood that gives them life and individuality.

"And hath made of one blood all nations of men for to dwell on all the face of the earth, and hath determined the times before appointed, and the bounds of their habitation." Acts 17:26.

Even though all human beings came from one blood, **adom**, in each blood is distinct genetic constitution that makes each one different from another such that no two people look alike, think alike, talk alike and have the same assignments. In fact, there are at least five physical features that make each one different from the other.

These are:

One, the thumb print. No two people have the same thumb print even if they are identical twins. Those printed marks on your thumb tell your life assignment and story. Anyone who can read those lines can tell your story in summary.

Two, the dental constitution. No two people have the same teeth constitution. Your set of teeth is just unique to you.

Three, the hair constitution. No two people have the same hair constitution. Your hairs are all numbered by God. ***"But the very hairs of your head are all numbered."*** Matt. 10:30.

Four, the skin configuration. No two people have the same skin configuration.

Five, the eyes make up. You don't look like any other human being so don't try to copy another human being thus you can lose your uniqueness and significance.

"As a bird that wandereth from her nest, so is a man that wandereth from his place." Prov. 27:8.

What is man that God is so mindful of him? It is because man is unique and different from all His other creations. Why are you different from angels and animals? You were made in God's image and likeness. Two qualities that make you different from all of God's creations and that is why God is so full of the thoughts of you.

"And God said, Let us make man in our image, after our likeness: and let them have dominion over the fish of the sea, and over the fowl of the air, and over the cattle, and over all the earth, and over every creeping thing that creepeth upon the earth." Gen. 1:26.

The word, *image*, Hebrew, **tselem** means a copy or exact duplicate representing some aspects of His perfection. Man was created by God to model some aspects of God. Each individual is designed by God to show forth an aspect of God. No individual has all of God's representations in its perfection except the Man Jesus Christ. Jesus is the only representation of the fullness of the Godhead in human form.

However, each one is a perfect representation of an aspect of God. That perfect side is what makes you look like God.

"For in Him the whole fullness of Deity (the Godhead) continues to dwell in bodily form [giving complete expression of the divine nature]." Col. 2:9. Amplified Version.

We can only become perfect expressions of God on earth when each one manifests the uniqueness of God in them as He has designed. So if you are designed to be God's yellow color, someone else is red color, another person green color, yet another person blue color, etc. All of us come together to form a rainbow of color manifesting the fullness of God in human form on earth. That is when we all can become the perfect human being God designed us to become. Perfection is achieved only when we all copy God in our uniqueness.

"He makes the whole body fit together perfectly. As each part does its own special work, it helps the other parts grow, so that the whole body is healthy and growing and full of love." Eph. 4:16. New Living Translation.

God designed you to be you by copying Him. You were designed to represent Him on earth. You were designed to show forth an aspect of God that only you can manifest. No other human being can show forth that aspect of God but you. This is why God is so mindful of you because of what He wants to show to His creation through you that He can only manifest through you. When you copy another human being, you lose that special privilege and thus frustrate God's purpose for you.

Like it happened to Judah and Benjamin in the time of Ezra when they had an awesome opportunity to build the house of God as commanded by a heathen king Cyrus, so it is happening to every human being. The Bible tells us that the people of the land worked hard to weaken the hands of the Israelites. The people of the land stirred up trouble, raised all kinds of accusations and even hired counselors to weaken their hands from fulfilling purpose.

"Then the people of the land weakened the hands of the people of Judah, and troubled them in building,

5 And hired counsellors against them, to frustrate their purpose, all the days of Cyrus king of Persia, even until the reign of Darius king of Persia.

6 And in the reign of Ahasuerus, in the beginning of his reign, wrote they unto him an accusation against the inhabitants of Judah and Jerusalem. " Ezra 4:4-6.

Right there in those verses, you can see how the enemies of your God assigned destiny work so hard to frustrate your divine purpose.

The word, **weaken**, Hebrew, **rapha**, means to slack; slow down; fail; cease; be feeble; to fall; to be left alone. This is what the enemy of your God assigned purpose will use people and situations to do to weaken you. You become sluggish in doing what you are supposed to do to fulfill your purpose. You become slack, slow, weak and feeble. You feel left alone and abandoned.

How did you get to this place where you are weakened? There is trouble you cannot understand or manage.

The word, *trouble*, Hebrew, **bahal**, means to make or cause to tremble inwardly. It also means to cause sudden alarm or agitation. It implies any situation that causes you to be in a haste or anxious. When suddenly you are agitated, alarmed and anxious, it can weaken you with time. It can cause you to fail or fall.

Beyond causing you trouble, the enemy can weaken you by stirring up accusations against you. People you know and don't know can accuse you of things you never thought or said or did. In fact, when they are saying things you never thought of or imagined, they can weaken you to the point of derailing you from your God assigned purpose.

Another thing the enemy can use to weaken you is hired counselors. These are people who are either hired by you or someone else to give you counsel and advice that will cause you to fail or fall. Be careful about who you listen to when you need advice. Anyone hired to counsel you are basically interested in their wages. When your colleagues, comrades and contemporaries give you advice, be careful.

"And God said, Let us make man in our image, after our likeness: and let them have dominion over the fish of the sea, and over the

fowl of the air, and over the cattle, and over all the earth, and over every creeping thing that creepeth upon the earth." Gen. 1:26.

The word, **likeness**, means resemblance or reflection. Man was created by God to look like God by looking at God. You were not designed by God to look like your parents or pastor. Every time you look like another human being, you are losing your uniqueness. If God needed a clone, He could have cloned man from the beginning. He designed you to look like Him by looking at Him. This is based on the law of reflection which states that when a ray of light reflects off a surface, the angle of reflection is equal to the angle of reflection. Based on this law, light reflects light when it falls on a surface that reflects it. You can say by this, what you see in front of a mirror is exactly what you see on the mirror. You can see yourself in a mirror just as you are.

You were designed by God to look like God by looking at Him daily. Man was never designed by God to look at himself or his environment to find success. He was designed to look at God and from God discover his significance and substance. As long as the first man Adam lived like this in the Garden of Eden, he was like God. He had the capacity of God to give names to all of God's creation as if it was God Himself. It was this capacity that gave him the wisdom and authority to dominate God's world because he was looking like God by looking at God. All creation responded to and obeyed man because they saw and heard God in man. You can now understand why creation obeyed our Lord Jesus Christ when He walked this earth. It was because He looked like the Father God so creation saw and heard God in Him.

"...What manner of man is this, that even the wind and the sea obey him?" Mark 4:41.

That question, *what manner of man is this*, still deserves an answer. The Old Testament Greek word for **man** has its root in the Greek word anthropos which means the upright upward looking being. Of all of God's creation, man was the only being that stood upright before God by looking at God. All other creations fell before God in obeisance. Man stood upright by looking at God. Man was never designed to be uptight but upright. He becomes uptight when he stops looking at God. Only man has been designed to be upright or righteous. Not even the angels in their glory can claim to be righteous.

From the moment man looked down at himself in the Garden of Eden, he lost his position of uprightness with God. You can't be looking down and survive the presence of God. As a result, man was kicked out of the Garden of God's delight. From that time, man struggles to get back to this place of uprightness. Unfortunately, he tries to earn it through so many other ways. Whereas the only way is to look at God so he can look like God. If you can determine to look at God on a daily basis, you can look like God to God's creation. This is a decision that no one can make for you but you.

This seven days journey is to help you look at the face of God daily for the next seven days.

The face of God is His word. It is not about a feeling of a presence. It is about seeing His face through the carvings and drawings we find in His word. His word gives us a clear outline and photograph of His person. This is the reason why Jesus never took pictures when He walked this earth because He did not want people to idolize the image when they can have the Person. Instead of a picture, He has given us His word which is His person written and expressed in ways that only the Holy Spirit can translate to become real in our experiences.

"In the beginning was the Word, and the Word was with God, and the Word was God.

2 The same was in the beginning with God.

3 All things were made by him; and without him was not any thing made that was made."
John 1:1-3.

COMMITMENT

Everything in life begins with a commitment. To sin begins with a commitment.

"He that committeth sin is of the devil; for the devil sinneth from the beginning. For this purpose the Son of God was manifested, that he might destroy the works of the devil. Whosoever is born of God doth not commit sin; for his seed remaineth in him: and he cannot sin, because he is born of God." 1 John 3:8-9.

For you to live right, requires commitment. You must decide to live right and take decisive steps. No one can make this choice for you.

"I call heaven and earth to record this day against you, that I have set before you life and death, blessing and cursing: therefore choose life, that both thou and thy seed may live."
Deut. 3019.

I dare you to make this commitment today by praying this prayer:

Dear Lord Jesus, I choose life and blessing today. I choose to change my world in the next seven days. I choose to change everything around me today. By this choice, I decide to look at Your face daily so that I can stand upright and never be uptight. I choose to spend quality time with You as I look at Your Word which is Your face. According to Your Word, may I be radically transformed by looking at

Your face in Your Word in the precious name of Jesus Christ my Lord and Master. Amen.

"But we all, with open face beholding as in a glass the glory of the Lord, are changed into the same image from glory to glory, even as by the Spirit of the Lord." 2 Cor. 3:18.

DAY ONE

For these seven days, we shall be looking at the face of God in Joel 2:21-27. In this scripture, there are instructions God has given to you and me that will shape us to look like Him.

The first instruction God gives us is: **FEAR NOT!**

That is a command not a suggestion.

Fear has been proven by medical science as the root cause of over eighty percent of all sickness and disease. In Luke 21:26, Jesus tells us that fear is what causes heart failure. Medical science confirms the failure of our body organs due to negative emotions like fear. As you begin this journey, you must get rid of fear from your heart.

Decide from today, **I WILL NOT BE AFRAID.** Shout it a thousand times a day.

Why FEAR NOT? Joel 2:21 says, **The Lord will do great things.** Yes, great things are about to happen to you that will suck up every fear in your being. Instead of looking at the things that cause you to be afraid, look at the great things God is doing behind the scenes that will become manifest soon.

Expect great things to happen to you from today. NO MORE FEAR!

"Fear not, O land; be glad and rejoice: for the LORD will do great things." Joel 2:21.

"And there shall be signs in the sun, and in the moon, and in the stars; and upon the earth distress of nations, with perplexity; the sea and the waves roaring;

Men's hearts failing them for fear, and for looking after those things which are coming on earth: for the powers of heaven shall be shaken.

And then shall they see the Son of man coming in a cloud with power and great glory.

And when these things begin to come to pass, then look up, and lift up your heads; for your redemption draweth nigh." Luke 21:25-28.

PRAYER: Lord, I choose to look up to You because my redemption comes from You. I take my eyes away from the signs and symptoms around me. My heart is strong because I see You at work in every area of my life in Jesus name. Amen.

PERSONAL EXERCISE

Take a look at your heart and life. Ask yourself, what are those things and people that are

making me afraid? What frightens me? Write
them down here:

1.

2.

3.

4.

5.

6.

7.

Now, look at all of them and tell yourself, I WILL NO MORE BE AFRAID of you any more in the name of my Lord and Master Jesus Christ. Amen.

"If thou shalt say in thine heart, These nations are more than I; how can I dispossess them?

18 Thou shalt not be afraid of them: but shalt well remember what the Lord thy God did unto Pharaoh, and unto all Egypt;

19 The great temptations which thine eyes saw, and the signs, and the wonders, and the mighty hand, and the stretched out arm, whereby the Lord thy God brought thee out: so shall the Lord thy God do unto all the people of whom thou art afraid.

20 Moreover the Lord thy God will send the hornet among them, until they that are left, and hide themselves from thee, be destroyed.

21 Thou shalt not be affrighted at them: for the Lord thy God is among you, a mighty God and terrible." Deut. 7:17-21.

DAY TWO

Get excited because it is a new day filled with great opportunities for you to enjoy God's best on earth. I really mean you should get excited to be alive to see this new day. I have died before but God in His mercy brought me back to life. So I appreciate life more than anyone. Every day I wake up, I shout, I AM ALIVE, THANK YOU JESUS. That alone gives the Devil and his gang a nervous breakdown.

As we hear God's command to FEAR NOT in Joel 2:21, I want us to demystify fear. Fear is simply the terror or threat of someone or something evil. It is the Serpent called Satan who has it from when he was thrown out of heaven. He lost out on God's glory.

When Adam bowed his knees to obey Satan, the same spirit of terror and timidity on Satan was passed on to man. From Gen. 3:10, the gene of man's being was possessed with fear. Man became a timid, threatened and terrorized being. That fear was the result of listening to the Serpent instead of the Spirit of God.

Man became conscious of his nakedness so he went to hide. Fear drives man to hide in all kinds of leaves like money, material things and other men. This same man God created naked and was not ashamed became a fear-filled being. Fear is the Devil's baggage you must not carry from this point on. Leave it for him. NO MORE FEAR!

"Now although the man and his wife were both naked, neither of them was embarrassed or ashamed." Gen 2:25. The Living Bible.

"And he said, I heard thy voice in the garden, and I was afraid, because I was naked; and I hid myself." Gen. 3:10.

PRAYER: Lord Jesus, You are my Savior and Master. I receive Your genetic constitution. I refuse the gene of fear that comes from the Serpent called Satan. I am God's seed. I am God's child. Fear is not in me. I have faith in God. NO MORE FEAR in me in Jesus name. Amen.

PERSONAL EXERCISE

Take a look at your life and ask yourself, who do I listen to that causes me to be filled with fear and shame? What do I listen to that causes me to feel ashamed and fearful? Write them down here:

1.

2.

3.

4.

5.

6.

7.

Now, make a decision that from henceforth, I WILL NOT LISTEN to these serpents around me. Lord, help me to be sensitive to know when the serpent called Satan is speaking through any human instrument in Jesus name. Help me to shut my ears and eyes to all they say and do in Jesus name. Amen.

"I will not be afraid of ten thousands of people, that have set themselves against me round about." Psalm 3:6.

"He will deliver you again and again so that no evil can touch you.

20 "He will keep you from death in famine and from the power of the sword in time of war.

21 "You will be safe from slander; no need to fear the future.

22 *"You shall laugh at war and famine; wild animals will leave you alone.*

23 *Dangerous animals will be at peace with you.*

24 *"You need not worry about your home while you are gone; nothing shall be stolen from your barns.*

25 *"Your sons shall become important men; your descendants shall be as numerous as grass!*

26 *You shall live a long, good life; like standing grain, you'll not be harvested until it's time!*

27 *I have found from experience that all of this is true. For your own good, listen to my counsel."* Job 5:19-27. The Living Bible.

DAY THREE

When God tells you one thing twice, it must be serious. In Joel 2:21, He commands you to **FEAR NOT**. In Joel 2:22, He commands you to **BE NOT AFRAID.** When you look at the bills for this month, your heart will almost be frightened. But God said, **DON'T BE AFRAID!**

Anyone or anything trying to put fear on you is already afraid of you or they have the spirit of fear that regulates them. You must not bow your knees to them so you don't catch what they are trying to offer you.

One secret to conquering your fear is knowing that what you are afraid of is taking

a risk on you hoping to succeed. You too must take a chance hoping to succeed.

When your hope is anchored on God's word, you can be rest assured that you will come out on the other side the winner. Even if you fail or fall, you will rise again. This is an assurance we have in Christ that non-believers don't have. Even if you die in the process, you are still a winner. Live or die, you win. This hope your opponent called Satan and his gang doesn't have. NO MORE FEAR!

"Fear not, my people; be glad now and rejoice, for he has done amazing things for you." Joel 2:21. The Living Bible.

"Be not afraid, ye beasts of the field: for the pastures of the wilderness do spring; for the tree beareth its fruit; the fig-tree and the vine yield full increase." Joel 2:22. Darby.

"And do not [for a moment] be frightened or intimidated in anything by your opponents and adversaries, for such [constancy and fearlessness] will be a clear sign (proof and seal) to them of [their impending] destruction, but [a sure token and evidence] of your deliverance and salvation, and that from God." Phil. 1:28. Amplified Version.

PRAYER: Father God, I believe and receive Your command to FEAR NOT. Therefore, I FEAR NOT. I refuse to be terrified by my opponents and all these bills I have seen. I have faith in the name of my Lord and Master Jesus

Christ to conquer every one of them. My confidence is in Your word and power at work in me. I declare that I AM MORE THAN A CONQUEROR IN JESUS NAME. AMEN.

PERSONAL EXERCISE

Take a look at all the bills and letters that are a threat to your being right now. Write them down here:

1.

2.

3.

4.

5.

6.

7.

Now, make a decision to obey God's command to **FEAR NOT**. Tell yourself, **I WILL NOT BE AFRAID** any more of these bills and threat letters, phone calls and text messages because God has commanded me to FEAR NOT. Like Hezekiah did in 2 Kings 19, Lord, I lay these letters and bills at Your feet. Do to these what You did to the king of Assyria in Jesus name. I have no fear in me because I believe God. The word of God works for me in Jesus name. Amen.

"And Hezekiah received the letter of the hand of the messengers, and read it: and Hezekiah went up into the house of the Lord, and spread it before the Lord.

15 And Hezekiah prayed before the Lord, and said, O Lord God of Israel, which dwellest between the cherubims, thou art the God, even thou alone, of all the kingdoms of the earth: thou hast made heaven and earth." 2 Kings 19:14-15.

"Therefore thus saith the Lord concerning the king of Assyria, He shall not come into this city, nor shoot an arrow there, nor come before it with shield, nor cast a bank against it.

33 By the way that he came, by the same shall he return, and shall not come into this city, saith the Lord.

34 For I will defend this city, to save it, for mine own sake, and for my servant David's sake." 2 Kings 19:32-34.

DAY FOUR

Three reasons why you must obey God's command when He said to you, **BE NOT AFRAID.** Joel 2:22.

One, your pastures will turn green again. Everything that turned brown because of the winter or heat will turn green again. Don't give up because your season is changing. A new season is coming. Life has seasons. There are two to four seasons every year. Don't be afraid of winter because summer is coming. Don't be afraid of summer because winter is coming. Seasons change.

Two, your trees will bear fruit again. You are a tree that produces its fruit in season. Your next fruit bearing season is here again. Don't commit any form of suicide whether spiritual or physical or academic or economic because a new season is coming. No season is permanent.

Three, your fig tree and vine will yield their strength. Your husband will bounce back again. Your wife will conceive again and this time she will bring forth that baby that will cause you to laugh again. You will find your mate. Why are you still afraid, worried and anxious? Stop it. In fact, slap yourself for letting yourself fear what is just passing by. NO MORE FEAR!

"Have no fear, you beasts of the field, for the grass-lands of the waste are becoming green, for the trees are producing fruit, the fig-tree and the vine give out their strength." Joel 2:22. Bible in Basic English.

"Blessed is the man that walketh not in the counsel of the ungodly, nor standeth in the way of sinners, nor sitteth in the seat of the scornful.

2 But his delight is in the law of the Lord; and in his law doth he meditate day and night.

And he shall be like a tree planted by the rivers of water, that bringeth forth his fruit in his season; his leaf also shall not wither; and whatsoever he doeth shall prosper." Psalm 1:1-3.

PRAYER: Lord, I believe and declare that **I AM BLESSED** because I fix my eyes on Your word concerning my family, finances, future and all that concerns me. Based on Your word, this is my season to bear fruit and I see fruits springing up from every corner for me. I shall

not wither. I shall not be disappointed. I AM
PROSPEROUS in Jesus name. Amen.

PERSONAL EXERCISE

Take a look at God's word again and begin to
consider the kinds of fruits you want to see from
today. List some here:

1.

2.

3.

4.

5.

6.

7.

Now, make a decision like Habakuk did in the face of drought to rejoice before the fruits manifest. Consider the fact that your rejoicing is your fixed deposit and payment for the fruits you will begin to see manifest from today in Jesus name. Amen.

"When I heard, my belly trembled; my lips quivered at the voice: rottenness entered into my bones, and I trembled in myself, that I might rest in the day of trouble: when he cometh up unto the people, he will invade them with his troops.

17 Although the fig tree shall not blossom, neither shall fruit be in the vines; the labour of the olive shall fail, and the fields shall yield no meat; the flock shall be cut off from the fold, and there shall be no herd in the stalls:

18 Yet I will rejoice in the Lord, I will joy in the God of my salvation.

19 The Lord God is my strength, and he will make my feet like hinds' feet, and he will make me to walk upon mine high places. To the chief singer on my stringed instruments." Hab. 3:16-19.

Lord, based on this word, I refuse to panic, tremble, worry or fear because of what I see or hear that is not looking like Your word to me. I choose to believe and confess Your word. I rejoice in Your word that is changing my situation to produce fruits for me. Thank You Lord Jesus for my harvest of blessings. Glory to God!

DAY FIVE

Whatever you do on this journey, do not think, talk or act fear because you have received a command from God to **FEAR NOT** and **BE NOT AFRAID**. Joel 2:21-22. It is a command you must obey. Be determined to obey God and no one else no matter their power, position or posture.

Do not allow what you see, read, feel or hear impose the Devil's nature of fear on your being. Fear is not a part of God's being. Lucifer had no fear of God when he worshiped God. That was why he thought up things that led to his downfall from heaven. Since he fell, fear has been his nature. When Adam obeyed his instruction in Eden, the same spirit of fear took over man's being. That is why you must never bow your knees to obey the enemy because you will end up taking his nature of fear. You become what you believe and bow to.

Thank God that in Christ we have been delivered from the fear of death. Fear is not in your gene as a new creation. Think, talk and act in obedience to God's word which we call faith, confidence in God's ability to perform His word in spite of your circumstances. NO MORE FEAR!

"For sin shall not [any longer] exert dominion over you, since now you are not under Law [as slaves], but under grace [as subjects of God's favor and mercy].

15 What then [are we to conclude]? Shall we sin because we live not under Law but under God's favor and mercy? Certainly not!

16 Do you not know that if you continually surrender yourselves to anyone to do his will, you are the slaves of him whom you obey, whether that be to sin, which leads to death, or to obedience which leads to righteousness (right doing and right standing with God)?

17 But thank God, though you were once slaves of sin, you have become obedient with all your heart to the standard of teaching in which you were instructed and to which you were committed.

18 And having been set free from sin, you have become the servants of righteousness (of conformity to the divine will in thought, purpose, and action)." Rom. 6:14-18. Amplified.

PRAYER: Lord Jesus, I stand on Your word that has set me free from the nature of Satan and sin. I refuse to be dominated by Satan, sickness and sin any more. I live by grace through faith in Your word in Jesus name. Amen.

PRACTICAL EXERCISE

When you look at your thoughts in line with God's word, ask yourself these questions:

1. What are the prevailing thoughts on my mind concerning men, money and material things?

2. What are the prevailing thoughts on my mind concerning healing, health and help?

3. What are the prevailing thoughts on my mind concerning marriage and ministry?

4. What are the prevailing thoughts on my mind concerning career and calling?

5. What are the prevailing thoughts on my mind concerning my purpose, position and possession?

"Then Peter and the apostles replied, We must obey God rather than men." Acts 5:29. Amplified.

Like Peter, Lord, I choose today to obey God rather than men. I put myself under the order and command of God as my Master. I refuse to subject myself to the order of men and my emotions. I am a new creature in Christ Jesus my Lord. Therefore, I live by faith in this life in Jesus name. Amen.

DAY SIX

The next instruction God has given us is: be glad and rejoice. Joel 2:21,23. To be glad here means to turn around with joy. This is not just a figure of speech. It is a prophetic act.

Stand up, turn around with joy because your situation is turning around for your good.

To rejoice means to brighten up your face. Wash your face very well. Don't allow those frowns that create lines in your face. Do this deliberately and be decisive about it.

You can be glad even in the face of danger just like what happened on our flight from Atlanta to

Lagos recently. The cabin crews were aware of a terrorist on board, yet they kept a bright face until the plane returned back and he was taken out. A journey of eleven hours now lasted two days. You can choose to panic and let the terrorist know you are afraid of what they can do to you or brighten up your face with courage and tell that sucker to go to hell.

God said, rejoice and be glad. I choose to obey God because eventually He will turn everything around for my good as I turn around with joy. Take a step of faith and just turn around with joy right now. NO MORE FEAR!

"Fear not, O land; be glad and rejoice: for the Lord will do great things.

23 Be glad then, ye children of Zion, and rejoice in the Lord your God: for he hath given you the former rain moderately, and he will cause to come down for you the rain, the former rain, and the latter rain in the first month." Joel 2:21,23.

PRAYER: Lord Jesus, today, I decide to rejoice and be glad. I refuse to allow my situation and other people decide my joy. It is my choice to rejoice and be glad. By faith in your word today, I am standing up and I am turning around with joy. As I turn around today, may my challenges and circumstances turn around for my good in Jesus name. Amen.

PERSONAL EXERCISE

Take a look at the things and people that make you lose your joy. List them down here:

1.

2.

3.

4.

5.

6.

7.

"This is the day which the Lord hath made; we will rejoice and be glad in it." Psalm 118:24.

"When I heard, my belly trembled; my lips quivered at the voice: rottenness entered into my bones, and I trembled in myself, that I might rest in the day of trouble: when he cometh up unto the people, he will invade them with his troops.

17 Although the fig tree shall not blossom, neither shall fruit be in the vines; the labour of the olive shall fail, and the fields shall yield no meat; the flock shall be cut off from the fold, and there shall be no herd in the stalls:

18 Yet I will rejoice in the Lord, I will joy in the God of my salvation.

19 The Lord God is my strength, and he will make my feet like hinds' feet, and he will make me to walk upon mine high places. To the chief singer on my stringed instruments." Hab 3:16-19.

DAY SEVEN

When God commands you to be glad and rejoice, He means for you to TURN AROUND WITH JOY and BRIGHTEN UP YOUR FACE. Joel 2:21,23.

Can you keep a bright face when you are 40,000 feet above sea level just one hour away from departure city with a terrorist on board? Thank God the pilot did not let us know exactly why the plane had to TURN AROUND to base. However, the cabin crew knew and they were still TURNING AROUND in the plane with joy and bright face. As soon as the plane landed, you can trust the United States. They can kill a fly with a machine gun. The reason they do that is so that in case they miss the target, the sights and sounds of them are just enough to cause their target a heart attack.

For one small fry, there were police and fire trucks on both sides and an invasion of police on our plane. That was enough to make the heart of that fine young man stop. Can you imagine when France sent 80,000 policemen after just two young men in Paris in 2015? Those boys died of heart attack before gun bullets got them down.

When all these bills start bumping at you from all directions and you don't know what to do, just TURN AROUND WITH JOY and BRIGHTEN UP YOUR FACE because God will TURN things around for your good. NO MORE FEAR!

"Fear not, earth! Be glad and celebrate! God has done great things.

23 Children of Zion, celebrate! Be glad in your God. He's giving you a teacher to train you how to live right — Teaching, like rain out of heaven, showers of words to refresh and nourish your soul, just as he used to do." Joel 2:21-23. THE MESSAGE.

PRAYER: Dear Lord Jesus, in obedience of Your command to me to turn around and brighten my face, I refuse to allow anything or anyone cause my face to frown today. Help me Lord to keep my eyes on You as You take care of me. I refuse to allow anything or anyone terrorize me anymore. I choose to walk in the confidence that You are with me, You are in me and You are for me in Jesus name. Amen.

PERSONAL EXERCISE

Take a look at your life and ask yourself these questions:

1. What are those things that terrorize me?

2. Who are those people that terrorize me?

3. What is it that causes my mind to wonder aimlessly?

4. What is it that makes me feel less than and inadequate for the day?

5. What can I do to change my present position so I don't have to be afraid any more?

6. Who can I talk with to gain the confidence I need to make quality progress from here?

7. Where can I go to daily to enhance my mind to succeed in my project?

"He shall deliver thee in six troubles: yea, in seven there shall no evil touch thee.

20 In famine he shall redeem thee from death: and in war from the power of the sword.

21 Thou shalt be hid from the scourge of the tongue: neither shalt thou be afraid of destruction when it cometh.

22 At destruction and famine thou shalt laugh: neither shalt thou be afraid of the beasts of the earth.

23 For thou shalt be in league with the stones of the field: and the beasts of the field shall be at peace with thee.

24 And thou shalt know that thy tabernacle shall be in peace; and thou shalt visit thy habitation, and shalt not sin.

25 Thou shalt know also that thy seed shall be great, and thine offspring as the grass of the earth.

26 Thou shalt come to thy grave in a full age, like as a shock of corn cometh in in his season.

*27 Lo this, we have searched it, so it is; hear it,
and know thou it for thy good."* Job 5:19-27.

WHY I CHOSE JESUS CHRIST?

Someone asked me many years ago, Mike, why did you accept Jesus Christ? I could have become an atheist, a Muslim, etc. Why Jesus Christ?

My answer to that question is for basically three reasons and the fourth one will blow your mind.

One, I accepted Jesus Christ because I needed a Father. A father is a life source. That means you came from him. According to the law of sustenance, you can only be sustained by your source. Fish came out of water and thus can only be sustained in a water environment. If you put it on land, no matter how nice looking, it will die in no distant time. I realized that God is my Source. I can only be sustained by Him. I discovered that I couldn't have a personal relationship with Him through any other one or way except through Jesus Christ. John 14:6. Acts 4:12.

Like a fish out of water in a land environment, you and I continue to struggle to survive until we reconnect with our natural habitat or source. This is God your Father. This happens only through Jesus Christ. You will never be fulfilled or become eternally relevant until you accept Jesus Christ into your heart as your personal Lord and Master. Then will you be able to connect with God your Source. Then will you know what it means to be sustained by the grace of God.

Two, I accepted Jesus Christ because I needed a friend. Man was designed to relate with his environment and people. Nobody can survive as an island. You will need friends in your life. For me, it is very easy to make friends. As I grew up, my life became messed up by the friends I had. Friends betrayed me. Some battered me. Yet some others left me each time after our relationship with bruises. The marks will always be there. It was my search unknown to me for the real friend that got me into such relationships. I did not know about the Friend that sticks closer than a brother. Proverbs 18:24.

Friends have scorned me like they did Job. Job's friends turned aside from him (Job 6:18). They laughed him to scorn (Job 12:4). He was such a laughing stock that his eyes poured out tears to God (Job 16:20). His kinfolks failed him. His friends forgot him (Job 19:14). I have been there.

I needed a friend who will love me the way I am. I found this Friend in Jesus. He is God who became Abraham's Friend (Gen. 18:17. 2 Chron. 20:7). What a Friend He was to Abraham that even when Abraham lied about his wife, God rebuked the king to restore Abraham's wife (Gen. 12:10-20. 20:1-18.). A true friend will be there for you in good times and bad ones. Jesus is the best Friend I have ever had in my life (John 15:14).

You will never know a true friend outside of Jesus Christ. Your parents? Spouse? Relatives? Classmates? Colleagues? I choose Jesus Christ because He will be there for me all the time. He said so and I believe Him.

Three, I needed a future. Life is past, present and future. I have seen the past, it was both good and bad. I cannot do anything about it. It is gone forever. I failed in the past. I did all the bad things in the past. But it is gone leaving me with the consequences of my wrong choices and deeds. Now I am in the present. What can I do to make the difference for my future? This is what I am concerned with today. I discovered that it is only in Jesus Christ that His precious blood washes my past away. My today is secured with His ever-abiding presence because He is a very present help. My tomorrow is taken care of because He told me not to worry about it.

I have a beautiful future in Jesus Christ because of what He did for me at the cross. I sinned and deserved to die. He took my sins and died in my place. In exchange, He gave me His very life, abundant life.

The fourth reason is that He changed my life. Religion tries to change people by principles, philosophies and practices. But Jesus came into my life without Him putting any demands on me to do things to earn His forgiveness. All He asked from me was to believe and receive Him. I did and found that my life is just changing everyday. When I started this journey, I did not look like what I am today. I am not the same every day. I can assure you that by tomorrow I will become better until the day when I shall be changed permanently at the sound of the trump of God. From that point, I will put on immortality and incorruption. Sin shall never have dominion over me for all eternity. Is this not the kind of life you really desire from the deepest part of your being?

Today, my friend, you must make up your mind to receive Jesus Christ or reject Him. It is your choice. If you want to choose Jesus Christ, it is easy. Just say out loud:

Jesus, I believe you came to this world because You love me. Your love constrained You to the cross where You died for my sins to be forgiven me. Jesus, I believe. Come into my heart today. Wash me with Your precious blood. Make me a new person whose love and passion will be for You the rest of my life on earth. Jesus, You are the Lord of my life from this day forward. Thank You for saving me in Jesus name. Amen.

If you have prayed this prayer, do write me today and I will send you some materials to help you in this journey to become all that God has designed you to be.

PARTNER WITH US

When God gives one man a vision, it will require the participation of several others to fulfill that vision. No single individual can carry out God's vision because God gives according to His size. Anyone who tries to fulfill God's vision by themselves either will get frustrated or finished off. In 1989, God told Brother Mike, *'Son, take this gospel and miracle power of the living Christ to the nations – impacting lives and destinies with the WORD.'* Since then, that word has been the driving force to reaching 30 million souls in at least 50 nations.

"And they beckoned unto their partners, which were in the other ship, that they should come and help them. And they came, and filled both the ships, so that they began to sink." Luke 5:7.

Through this message, we are beckoning on you to come alongside with us through your support and partnership. Help us reach millions around the world. Help us to fill our boat with a massive harvest. The beauty of this partnership is that when you help us, our boat and your boat will be filled. Together, we shall have a net breaking and boat sinking harvest.

Three things you CAN do to help us:

1. You can PRAY. Zech. 10:1. Acts 4:28-30. Eph. 6:18-20. Your prayers travel faster than the speed of light. You can commit to pray for us on a regular basis.

2. You can PLANT your seed of any size. Your money or material seed is the mobile force that moves the gospel from person to person and place to place. Your money or material is YOU

GOing places you may not have the chance to be physically. Give generously. You can give your offering and seeds with your credit or debit card with this email address: *amamieye@yahoo.co.uk* through *https://www.pay.google.com* or MAWO account details:

GTBank account number 0038894924. If you are outside Nigeria, you can give through MoneyGram.com for free. GTBank accepts money through MoneyGram for free. Use it while the opportunity last.

In Nigeria, you can give by using your bank code as follows:

For offering, dial: *bankcode*000*491+amount#

For tithes, dial: *bankcode*000*492+amount#

If you are using GTBank for instance, your bank code is 737, so you can dial: *737*000*491+amount#

If you are in the United States of America, you can give your offering to Bank of America account number 0905418443. ABA Routing number is: 121000358.

With Zelle, send to: **amamieye@yahoo.co.uk**

If you are in the United Kingdom, you can give your offering to NatWest Bank account number 52344819. Sort code 602112.

3. You can PARTICIPATE with us as you join forces with us in any location near you. I look forward to see you as we gather together a net breaking and boat sinking harvest. Luke 5:7. If you hear a voice saying, ignore this message, just know that it is the old serpent from the Garden. Tell that voice to shut up because you are the sheep of Jesus and you only obey the voice of your Master Jesus Christ. John 10:27. Thank you very much for obeying His voice in your heart and for being a part of what God is doing with us around the nations.

FOR MORE INFORMATION

Send in your testimonies to let us know how this devotional has been a blessing to you.

Send in your prayer requests as well.

Stand with us to help us reach thirty million souls in fifty nations.

For more spiritual help, counseling and prayer ministration, contact:

Bishop Michael O. Amamieye
Michael Amamieye Word Outreach, International

a/k/a Aggressive Faith Ministries
Plot 13 Walter Akpana Lay Out off 394 Ikwerre
Road Mile 5 Rumueprikom, P. O. Box 12378, Port
Harcourt, Nigeria.

Hotlines: +2348050987377, +234901800MAWO
WhatsApp: +2348036732188

U.S.A: +19162456157
www.aggressivefaith.org
E-mail: info@aggressivefaith.org

ABOUT THE AUTHOR

Psalm 40:2,3 is a keynote to the life and ministry of Michael O. Amamieye. He was radically saved, healed and delivered from the power of darkness that endangered his youth. He is a living proof of God's matchless and abundant grace.

Since 1983, Brother Mike has been president, pastor and pioneer of several fellowships, churches and movements. He is instrumental in birthing many sons and daughters unto glory. He is a consecrated bishop with an oversight that reaches five continents.

In 1984, the Lord called Brother Mike to world evangelism with a mandate to *take the gospel and miracle power of the risen Christ to the nations – impacting lives and destinies with the WORD!* He is the President of **Michael Amamieye Word Outreach International** *also known as* **Aggressive Faith Ministries** with headquarters in the Garden City of Port Harcourt, Nigeria. He is the President of **Intensive Ministers Training School**. He is the Chairman of **Aggressive Faith Publishing Company**. Through this ministry, Brother Mike is determined to reach at least thirty million souls in at least fifty nations with the simple proclamation of the gospel of Christ with evidence that brings salvation, healing, deliverance, blessing and joy.

An evangelist by calling, he is a graduate of the **Billy Graham School of Evangelism**. He is a member of **Proclamation Evangelism Network** and an associate evangelist with the

Global Network of Evangelists founded by the **Luis Palau Association**. He has been interviewed on **Decision Today** Radio broadcast and **Decision** magazine both of which are owned by the **Billy Graham Evangelistic Association.** He has also appeared on GODTV as well as several other networks around the world.

Bishop Mike is a member of the **International Communion of Charismatic Churches** founded by the late Archbishop Benson Idahosa and several others. He has been honored in a public ceremony where the Mayor of the city of East Cleveland, Ohio gave him the key to the city in 2003. **LEADS Africa** honored him as an icon of nation building in 2012. **The Voice** magazine in Holland honored him with the spiritual leadership award in 2014. In 2019, he was awarded an honorary doctorate degree by

Triune Biblical University in New York. He is on high demand in crusades, conferences and conventions around the world.

He is the author of more than twenty books. He is a prolific and thought captivating writer with many of his works published in newsletters, magazines and newspapers around the world.

Bishop Mike is happily married to Princess Monivi, an ordained minister of the gospel and a health consultant. They are blessed with two biological children, Edwina Aleme and Mehetabel Favour as well as many others.